Manifesting Your Destiny

A Guide to Understanding the Four Stages of Process

Rhonda Pettigrew

Manifesting Your Destiny
Copyright © 2013 by Rhonda Pettigrew

All rights reserved. No part of this book may be reproduced or transmitted in any form or by any means without written permission from the author.

ISBN 978-0-692-61544-7

Printed in USA by Destiny Publishing, Jackson, Tennessee

Dedication and Acknowledgements

I am convinced that every accomplishment is a result of a corporate effort and a strong support base.

So, first of all, I want to thank my husband, Pastor Danny Pettigrew, and dedicate this book to him for his continual display of love, support, and patience as I pursue the assignments of God for my life. I, also, thank my mother, Faye, my sisters, Sophia and Anita, and my entire family who supports me in everything that I do.

Special thanks to the Destiny Church congregation for allowing me to serve you while sowing into the world.

All of you are helping me to Manifest My Destiny!

Table of Contents

Introduction 7

Chapter 1 11
Incubation Stage

Chapter 2 29
Preparation Stage

Chapter 3 41
Excavation Stage

Chapter 4 57
Activation Stage

Introduction

Most people struggle in the areas of destiny and purpose. The biggest issue is that destiny demands fulfillment, whereas purpose demands expression. Purpose without destiny yields a stagnant life, leaving many people frustrated. There is, absolutely, no way that you can reach your maximum potential operating from a place of frustration.

One misconception is that regardless of what is done, you will eventually fulfill your destiny. However, the truth is where you are today is a direct result of decisions that you made in the past. Destiny is not forced. It is a matter of choice. The good news is that if you are not pleased with where you are, you can make a decision to change it, starting today.

God created you with destiny and purpose in mind.

> ***Jeremiah 29:11***
>
> *King James Version (KJV)*
> *¹¹ For I know the thoughts that I think toward you, saith the L*ORD*, thoughts of peace, and not of evil, to give you an expected end.*

Your expected end in the Hebrew translation is *tiqvah*, meaning expectation, or things hoped for. Therefore, your expected end is the place that your faith will allow you to believe and seize.

> ***Romans 12:3***
>
> *King James Version (KJV)*
>
> *³ For I say, through the grace given unto me, to every man that is among you, not to think of himself more highly than he ought to think; but to think soberly, according as God hath dealt to every man the measure of faith.*

The measure of faith in this scripture refers to capacity. It is up to you to increase your faith capacity. Although mustard seed faith is where you start, you cannot manifest the fullness of your destiny with mustard seed faith. The way to increase your capacity is with the Word of God. The bible says that faith comes by hearing and hearing the Word of God. It is vitally important that you grow into a place of faith that yields success by the teaching, reading, and applying of the Word of God.

Your destiny is not predicated on your last name, or economic status. It is, also, bigger than a negative word spoken over your life, lack of affirmation, depression, hurt, or pain. Your destiny is rooted in Christ, and He reveals it do you. However, revelation is birthed out of relationship with Jesus Christ.

To "manifest" means to make something evident in the world. Manifesting your destiny means more than achieving dreams and goals. The deeper definition of destiny is revealing to yourself your life's purpose and sharing it with the world. When you manifest your destiny, you reveal your potential to yourself, first, and, then, to the world.

However, you must make a decision to embrace the process, which is just as important as the destination. There are times during the process that you will feel overwhelmed, ashamed, or tired. However, you must continue on. What looks like a setback is really a setup for an accelerated comeback. Also, it is during these times that God is working in and on you, using your process to bless someone else. Destiny is never assigned with one person in mind. There are people that are strategically placed in your life to benefit from your process, and, ultimately, God gets the glory. So, it is crucial to you, as well as everyone tied to you, that you do not abort your process.

As you navigate through this book, you will find the benefits in the stages of your process and gain the strength to continue to trust God as you move closer to **"Manifesting your Destiny."**

# Chapter One

The Incubation Stage

Chapter One
Incubation Stage

God reveals the details of destiny to you at the right times. Sometimes, it is more beneficial for your destiny to remain hidden from you for a season because if you could see it, you would sabotage it, consciously or unconsciously. The reason is because it can be a hard struggle when your purpose is in seed form. When a seed is planted, it has to die and grow down before any type of growth up is visible. It is the same with your destiny. There are times that it appears to be inactivity, but you are actually on track. You cannot confuse the lack of visibility for inactivity. God is always working, even when you cannot see it, or feel Him.

Incubation is the gradual development of something in an interior environment until it is fully developed. When a mother gives birth to a premature baby, the baby has to be incubated to help with the development and to minimize infections. The same thing is true with your destiny. During the incubation stage, there is a risk that your destiny and purpose can become contaminated, so God has it protected while He grows, develops, and matures you. That is why it is extremely dangerous to look at where people are at one moment and try size up their destiny based on their present reality. Also, as you begin to understand this stage in the process, you will no longer become distraught when other people do not recognize who you are. Your mentality has to be that if they don't know right away, eventually they will!

The understanding of this stage will take away feeling of jealousy, as well as measuring, and comparing yourself with someone else's plight. There must be an awareness of where you are in the process. Your destiny just may be in seed form, whereas, other people may be in another stage of the process.

One thing is certain at all times. You can be comforted in knowing that God is working some unimaginable things through you, even when you don't see the entire picture. Ephesians 3:20 says that He will do exceeding abundantly above all that we ask or think.

In the incubation stage of your destiny, you are vulnerable to predators and pestilence—sickness and disease. It is the plan of the enemy to contaminate you before you develop, so that your destiny and purpose will not come into fruition. Many things that you are falling short of now come from seeds planted by the enemy in your early childhood years or early stages of the process of destiny fulfillment. Therefore, there are two things must take place in this stage to further your development. You must be environmentally protected and nutritionally fed.

Many insecurities, or things that you are falling short of, could stem from early contamination. When the enemy sees great potential in someone, he tries to kill them in the infancy stage. Herod tried to kill Jesus when He was born, and Pharaoh set out to kill all the first-born male babies because of Moses' destiny.

> *Matthew 13:24-30 says,*
>
> *24 Another parable put he forth unto them, saying, The kingdom of heaven is likened unto a man which sowed good seed in his field:*
>
> *25 But while men slept, his enemy came and sowed tares among the wheat, and went his way.*
>
> *26 But when the blade was sprung up, and brought forth fruit, then appeared the tares also.*
>
> *27 So the servants of the householder came and said unto him, Sir, didst not*

thou sow good seed in thy field? from whence then hath it tares?

²⁸ He said unto them, An enemy hath done this. The servants said unto him, Wilt thou then that we go and gather them up?

²⁹ But he said, Nay; lest while ye gather up the tares, ye root up also the wheat with them.

³⁰ Let both grow together until the harvest: and in the time of harvest I will say to the reapers, Gather ye together first the tares, and bind them in bundles to burn them: but gather the wheat into my barn.

There are some things in you that have to be separated by God later in your process. If the separating would have been done too soon, it would have killed you, or pieces of your destiny would have been aborted because the issues were connected to the root.

Sometimes, you don't know what you are contaminated with until you start walking in purpose. At that moment, you find yourself making statements like, "I was doing fine, and then all of a sudden this issue came up out of nowhere." Actually, it was there all along, but it was disguised or suppressed.

As you continue in the process, you must, continually, remind yourself that the enemy does not waste his time on unproductive people, and he really launches an attack when you start growing in God.

Seeds of infection in the Incubation Stage are neglect, abuse, and rejection. In 2 Samuel 4, Mephibosheth was neglected and dropped by his nurse and left crippled. This neglect caused him to be insecure. Even though he was a prince, son of Jonathan and the grandson to King Saul, he settled for living in Lodebar.

Many people have been crippled with neglect, leaving a seed of insecurity that has caused them to settle for a life less than what God has intended.

Uncontrolled anger, sexual immorality, and insecurity are an indication of contamination. Exodus 2, says that Moses' mother saw that he was a goodly child, so she sent down the river. Pharaoh's daughter took the child and raised him as her own. Even though, Moses' mother thought that she was doing what was best for him, he still was contaminated with a seed of neglect that later caused his uncontrolled anger to be displayed by smiting the rock, causing him to forfeit entrance to the promised land, Canaan.

When you look at the life of King David, you find that he faced a seed of rejection. Can you imagine not being considered as eligible to be king by your natural father, or being overlooked because of your physical appearance? This is the story of many. This seed of rejection later caused David to have to deal with sexual immorality and murder. He committed adultery with Uriah's wife, and later killed him to cover it up.

In order to be free from this contamination, you must be environmentally protected during the early development of your purpose. There are some places that you will not be able to go, and people that you will not be able to have close relationship with. In order to grow, you must place yourself in an environment that is conducive for the growth of your seed of purpose.

Also, you have to be nutritionally fed. In other words, you need digest the Word of God and positive, faith-filled words only. You cannot jeopardize your future taking in or speaking negative words over your life.

With this protection in place, you are well on your way to **"Manifesting your Destiny."**

Incubation Stage Quote:

> *You can be comforted in knowing that God is working some unimaginable things through you, even when you don't see the entire picture.*

Notes:

Chapter Two

The Preparation Stage

Chapter Two
Preparation Stage

It was proven in the Incubation Stage that everything God allowed you to go through, the good and the bad, was preparing you for your future. Every negative word, every form of abuse, and every setback is still a part of preparation. However, purpose prevails after preparation.

When you study the life of Joseph, you will find that opposition was really preparation for success.

Genesis 50:19-20
King James Version (KJV)

[19] And Joseph said unto them, Fear not: for am I in the place of God?

20 But as for you, ye thought evil against me; but God meant it unto good, to bring to pass, as it is this day, to save much people alive.

To "prepare" means to make ready beforehand for a purpose, or activity, to put into a proper state of mind, to work out the details of or to put together.

Preparation is vital to success. We often wait on elevation or an accomplishment to happen before we get everything together. When, instead, God's way is to prepare and operate like you already have the blessing. You can easily hold up the next stage in your process to your destiny with a lack of preparation.

In Genesis 1, you find that God prepared elements and systems before He formed man in Genesis 2. We are made in the image of God; therefore, the power to prepare is on the inside of us. Every person has a seed of discipline on the inside that can be tapped into and extracted.

There are four principles that we can take from Joseph's process in Genesis 37. First of all, he was hated by his brothers. In this stage, you have to become comfortable with the fact that everyone will not celebrate you and what you are doing.

Secondly, Joseph was placed in a pit. The principle in this is that sometimes you have to experience a low place to show the ones that put you there that favor is uncontainable.

Thirdly, Joseph was imprisoned. Many of you fall into situations where you feel trapped. However, it is in this stage that you get the revelation that your external circumstances do not determine your freedom. You can be free in your spirit and your mind, but trapped in an undesirable situation.

Lastly, Joseph interpreted dreams while he was in prison. God, often times, will place you in a position where you are assigned to assist someone else towards their destiny while waiting on the manifestation of your own. Making things happen for someone else is sowing a seed toward your destiny. You may be called to pastor, but currently serving as a worship leader or armor bearer. You may desire to own a business, but sometimes you have to start your preparation in the mail room. It does not take anything from who you are. Be confident in knowing that the servanthood principle is preparing you for your next place.

Preparation Stage Quote:

> *Preparation is vital to success. You can easily hold up the next stage in your process to your destiny with a lack of preparation.*

Notes:

Chapter Three

The Excavation Stage

Chapter Three
Excavation Stage

Excavation is the discovery, exposing, or uncovering by digging. Spiritually, it is the process of discovering and unearthing valuable resources for the benefit of mankind and the Kingdom of God.

Genesis 2:1-15

King James Version (KJV)

2 Thus the heavens and the earth were finished, and all the host of them.

² And on the seventh day God ended his work which he had made; and he rested on the seventh day from all his work which he had made.

3 And God blessed the seventh day, and sanctified it: because that in it he had rested from all his work which God created and made.

4 These are the generations of the heavens and of the earth when they were created, in the day that the L<small>ORD</small> God made the earth and the heavens,

5 And every plant of the field before it was in the earth, and every herb of the field before it grew: for the L<small>ORD</small> God had not caused it to rain upon the earth, and there was not a man to till the ground.

6 But there went up a mist from the earth, and watered the whole face of the ground.

7 And the L<small>ORD</small> God formed man of the dust of the ground, and breathed into his nostrils the breath of life; and man became a living soul.

8 And the L<small>ORD</small> God planted a garden eastward in Eden; and there he put the man whom he had formed.

⁹ And out of the ground made the L{\sc ord} God to grow every tree that is pleasant to the sight, and good for food; the tree of life also in the midst of the garden, and the tree of knowledge of good and evil.

¹⁰ And a river went out of Eden to water the garden; and from thence it was parted, and became into four heads.

¹¹ The name of the first is Pison: that is it which compasseth the whole land of Havilah, where there is gold;

¹² And the gold of that land is good: there is bdellium and the onyx stone.

¹³ And the name of the second river is Gihon: the same is it that compasseth the whole land of Ethiopia.

¹⁴ And the name of the third river is Hiddekel: that is it which goeth toward the east of Assyria. And the fourth river is Euphrates.

¹⁵ And the L{\sc ord} God took the man, and put him into the garden of Eden to dress it and to keep it.

In Genesis 2, the river Pison in the Hebrew translation is "increase." The river Gihon is "bursting forth." The river Hiddekel is "rapid, quick, or sudden." The river Euphrates is "fruitfulness." God surrounded man in the garden with increase, bursting forth, rapidly with fruitfulness.

When God spoke earth into creation, everything that went into it was valuable. Therefore, when God formed man, He used the most valuable element He created, with was earth. You were created in the image and likeness of God and formed by the most valuable element.

On earth, diamonds are extremely valuable, but they are hidden under the surface. In order to acquire them, miners have to dig deep and chisel through hard surfaces. Then, when they find it, the product does not look the way it will in its finished state. In the beginning, it is coal, but after it is processed, it is a diamond.

Metaphorically, your destiny is the same. Your process can consist of digging deep and chiseling through some calloused areas to extract the valuable assets inside of you.

You can rest assured in knowing that just because your destiny is in its coal state, the diamond will be revealed after your process.

The value of an extracted resource is measured by the rareness of its quantity and by the extremity of the process by which it is obtained.

You may be thinking that your process seems worse than everyone around you. That could be an indication of how extremely valuable you are to God, and how much purpose you are carrying. When you understand this, you will appreciate the excavation stage in your journey towards your destiny.

Just as everything we need is in the earth, i.e. water, air, oxygen. Everything you need to manifest your destiny is already on the inside of you. It just needs to be excavated. God did not make an incomplete earth, and neither did He make an incomplete person. Therefore, another person does not complete you. You were made complete by God, the Father.

2 Corinthians 4:7 says that we have this treasure in earthen vessels, that the excellency of the power may be of God, and not of us.

2 Corinthians 4:7

The Message (MSG)

7-12 If you only look at us, you might well miss the brightness. We carry this precious Message around in the unadorned clay pots of our ordinary lives. That's to prevent anyone from confusing God's incomparable power with us. As it is, there's not much chance of that. You know for yourselves that we're not much to look at. We've been surrounded and battered by troubles, but we're not demoralized; we're not sure what to do, but we know that God knows what to do; we've been spiritually terrorized, but God hasn't left our side; we've been thrown down, but we haven't broken. What they did to Jesus, they do to us—trial and torture, mockery and murder; what Jesus did among them, he does in us—he lives! Our lives are at constant risk for Jesus' sake, which makes Jesus' life all the more evident in us. While we're going through the worst, you're getting in on the best!

God has done something for us, *salvation*, so that He can do something in us *sanctification*, so that He might do something through us, *the work of ministry.*

Genesis 1:11-12

King James Version (KJV)

¹¹ And God said, Let the earth bring forth grass, the herb yielding seed, and the fruit tree yielding fruit after his kind, whose seed is in itself, upon the earth: and it was so.

¹² And the earth brought forth grass, and herb yielding seed after his kind, and the tree yielding fruit, whose seed was in itself, after his kind: and God saw that it was good.

Luke 17:20-21

King James Version (KJV)

²⁰ And when he was demanded of the Pharisees, when the kingdom of God should come, he answered them and said, The kingdom of God cometh not with observation:

²¹ Neither shall they say, Lo here! or, lo there! for, behold, the kingdom of God is within you.

The Kingdom of God is within you! Everything you need to fulfill destiny and purpose is within you!

Excavation Stage Quote:

> *Everything you need to manifest your destiny is already on the inside of you.*

Notes:

Chapter Four

Activation Stage

Chapter Four
Activation Stage

Activation is the culmination of Divine timing and human willingness to be used by God for His glory and to meet a Kingdom need.

In this stage you must be willing to demonstrate:

1. A willingness to run to what others run from

2. Obedience by following instructions without complete understanding

3. A lifestyle of Fasting and praying

4. Prophetic Utterances and Decrees

Willingness to Run to What Others Run From

In order to manifest the destiny that lies inside of you, you cannot be afraid of what is ahead. There has to be an execution of your faith with a confidence that you will be victorious over any obstacle in your path. In 1 Samuel 17, David's experiences with God had grown him to a point that no giant was too big to come down.

1 Samuel 17

King James Version (KJV)

17 Now the Philistines gathered together their armies to battle, and were gathered together at Shochoh, which belongeth to Judah, and pitched between Shochoh and Azekah, in Ephesdammim.

2 And Saul and the men of Israel were gathered together, and pitched by the valley of Elah, and set the battle in array against the Philistines.

3 And the Philistines stood on a mountain on the one side, and Israel stood on a mountain on the other side: and there was a valley between them.

4 And there went out a champion out of the camp of the Philistines, named Goliath, of Gath, whose height was six cubits and a span.

5 And he had an helmet of brass upon his head, and he was armed with a coat of mail; and the weight of the coat was five thousand shekels of brass.

6 And he had greaves of brass upon his legs, and a target of brass between his shoulders.

7 And the staff of his spear was like a weaver's beam; and his spear's head weighed six hundred shekels of iron: and one bearing a shield went before him.

8 And he stood and cried unto the armies of Israel, and said unto them, Why are ye come out to set your battle in array? am not I a Philistine, and ye servants to Saul? choose you a man for you, and let him come down to me.

9 If he be able to fight with me, and to kill me, then will we be your servants: but if I prevail against him, and kill him, then shall ye be our servants, and serve us.

10 And the Philistine said, I defy the armies of Israel this day; give me a man, that we may fight together.

11 When Saul and all Israel heard those words of the Philistine, they were dismayed, and greatly afraid.

12 Now David was the son of that Ephrathite of Bethlehemjudah, whose name was Jesse; and he had eight sons: and the man went among men for an old man in the days of Saul.

13 And the three eldest sons of Jesse went and followed Saul to the battle: and the names of his three sons that went to the battle were Eliab the firstborn, and next unto him Abinadab, and the third Shammah.

14 And David was the youngest: and the three eldest followed Saul.

15 But David went and returned from Saul to feed his father's sheep at Bethlehem.

16 And the Philistine drew near morning and evening, and presented himself forty days.

17 And Jesse said unto David his son, Take now for thy brethren an ephah of this parched corn, and these ten loaves, and run to the camp of thy brethren;

18 And carry these ten cheeses unto the captain of their thousand, and look how thy brethren fare, and take their pledge.

19 Now Saul, and they, and all the men of Israel, were in the valley of Elah, fighting with the Philistines.

20 And David rose up early in the morning, and left the sheep with a keeper, and took, and went, as Jesse had commanded him; and he came to the trench, as the host was going forth to the fight, and shouted for the battle.

21 For Israel and the Philistines had put the battle in array, army against army.

22 And David left his carriage in the hand of the keeper of the carriage, and ran into the army, and came and saluted his brethren.

23 And as he talked with them, behold, there came up the champion, the Philistine of Gath, Goliath by name, out of the armies of the Philistines, and spake according to the same words: and David heard them.

24 And all the men of Israel, when they saw the man, fled from him, and were sore afraid.

25 And the men of Israel said, Have ye seen this man that is come up? surely to defy Israel is he come up: and it shall be, that the man who killeth him, the king will enrich him with great riches, and will give him his daughter, and make his father's house free in Israel.

26 And David spake to the men that stood by him, saying, What shall be done to the man that killeth this Philistine, and taketh away the reproach from Israel? for who is this uncircumcised Philistine, that he should defy the armies of the living God?

²⁷ And the people answered him after this manner, saying, So shall it be done to the man that killeth him.

²⁸ And Eliab his eldest brother heard when he spake unto the men; and Eliab's anger was kindled against David, and he said, Why camest thou down hither? and with whom hast thou left those few sheep in the wilderness? I know thy pride, and the naughtiness of thine heart; for thou art come down that thou mightest see the battle.

²⁹ And David said, What have I now done? Is there not a cause?

³⁰ And he turned from him toward another, and spake after the same manner: and the people answered him again after the former manner.

³¹ And when the words were heard which David spake, they rehearsed them before Saul: and he sent for him.

³² And David said to Saul, Let no man's heart fail because of him; thy servant will go and fight with this Philistine.

33 And Saul said to David, Thou art not able to go against this Philistine to fight with him: for thou art but a youth, and he a man of war from his youth.

34 And David said unto Saul, Thy servant kept his father's sheep, and there came a lion, and a bear, and took a lamb out of the flock:

35 And I went out after him, and smote him, and delivered it out of his mouth: and when he arose against me, I caught him by his beard, and smote him, and slew him.

36 Thy servant slew both the lion and the bear: and this uncircumcised Philistine shall be as one of them, seeing he hath defied the armies of the living God.

37 David said moreover, The LORD that delivered me out of the paw of the lion, and out of the paw of the bear, he will deliver me out of the hand of this Philistine. And Saul said unto David, Go, and the LORD be with thee.

38 And Saul armed David with his armour, and he put an helmet of brass upon his head; also he armed him with a coat of mail.

³⁹ And David girded his sword upon his armour, and he assayed to go; for he had not proved it. And David said unto Saul, I cannot go with these; for I have not proved them. And David put them off him.

⁴⁰ And he took his staff in his hand, and chose him five smooth stones out of the brook, and put them in a shepherd's bag which he had, even in a scrip; and his sling was in his hand: and he drew near to the Philistine.

⁴¹ And the Philistine came on and drew near unto David; and the man that bare the shield went before him.

⁴² And when the Philistine looked about, and saw David, he disdained him: for he was but a youth, and ruddy, and of a fair countenance.

⁴³ And the Philistine said unto David, Am I a dog, that thou comest to me with staves? And the Philistine cursed David by his gods.

44 And the Philistine said to David, Come to me, and I will give thy flesh unto the fowls of the air, and to the beasts of the field.

45 Then said David to the Philistine, Thou comest to me with a sword, and with a spear, and with a shield: but I come to thee in the name of the LORD of hosts, the God of the armies of Israel, whom thou hast defied.

46 This day will the LORD deliver thee into mine hand; and I will smite thee, and take thine head from thee; and I will give the carcases of the host of the Philistines this day unto the fowls of the air, and to the wild beasts of the earth; that all the earth may know that there is a God in Israel.

47 And all this assembly shall know that the LORD saveth not with sword and spear: for the battle is the LORD's, and he will give you into our hands.

48 And it came to pass, when the Philistine arose, and came, and drew nigh to meet David, that David hastened, and ran toward the army to meet the Philistine.

⁴⁹ And David put his hand in his bag, and took thence a stone, and slang it, and smote the Philistine in his forehead, that the stone sunk into his forehead; and he fell upon his face to the earth.

⁵⁰ So David prevailed over the Philistine with a sling and with a stone, and smote the Philistine, and slew him; but there was no sword in the hand of David.

⁵¹ Therefore David ran, and stood upon the Philistine, and took his sword, and drew it out of the sheath thereof, and slew him, and cut off his head therewith. And when the Philistines saw their champion was dead, they fled.

⁵² And the men of Israel and of Judah arose, and shouted, and pursued the Philistines, until thou come to the valley, and to the gates of Ekron. And the wounded of the Philistines fell down by the way to Shaaraim, even unto Gath, and unto Ekron.

⁵³ And the children of Israel returned from chasing after the Philistines, and they spoiled their tents.

54 And David took the head of the Philistine, and brought it to Jerusalem; but he put his armour in his tent.

55 And when Saul saw David go forth against the Philistine, he said unto Abner, the captain of the host, Abner, whose son is this youth? And Abner said, As thy soul liveth, O king, I cannot tell.

56 And the king said, Enquire thou whose son the stripling is.

57 And as David returned from the slaughter of the Philistine, Abner took him, and brought him before Saul with the head of the Philistine in his hand.

58 And Saul said to him, Whose son art thou, thou young man? And David answered, I am the son of thy servant Jesse the Bethlehemite.

Obedience in Following Instructions without Complete Instructions

In Genesis 12, God speaks to Abram and gives him instructions that are impossible to carry out without faith and trust in God. During your journey, every specific detail may not be revealed to you. However, the end will be made clear by God. You must maintain faith and trust in God to make it through the middle. There cannot be any other options outside of obedience. To receive uncommon favor, many times you have to obey uncommon instructions.

Genesis 12:1-3

King James Version (KJV)

12 Now the LORD had said unto Abram, Get thee out of thy country, and from thy kindred, and from thy father's house, unto a land that I will shew thee:

2 And I will make of thee a great nation, and I will bless thee, and make thy name great; and thou shalt be a blessing:

3 And I will bless them that bless thee, and curse him that curseth thee: and in thee shall all families of the earth be blessed.

Fasting and Praying

Daniel 10:11-13

King James Version (KJV)

¹¹ And he said unto me, O Daniel, a man greatly beloved, understand the words that I speak unto thee, and stand upright: for unto thee am I now sent. And when he had spoken this word unto me, I stood trembling.

¹² Then said he unto me, Fear not, Daniel: for from the first day that thou didst set thine heart to understand, and to chasten thyself before thy God, thy words were heard, and I am come for thy words.

¹³ But the prince of the kingdom of Persia withstood me one and twenty days: but, lo, Michael, one of the chief princes, came to help me; and I remained there with the kings of Persia.

You must maintain a continual lifestyle of fasting and praying to experience a free flow of exchange between you and God.

Prophetic Utterances and Decrees

Job 22:27-29

King James Version (KJV)

²⁷ Thou shalt make thy prayer unto him, and he shall hear thee, and thou shalt pay thy vows.

²⁸ Thou shalt also decree a thing, and it shall be established unto thee: and the light shall shine upon thy ways.

²⁹ When men are cast down, then thou shalt say, There is lifting up; and he shall save the humble person.

Prophetic words, or their timing, are conditioned upon you taking certain steps of obedience.

The prophetic is designed to stir and cause destiny to come alive in you, so you will become passionate about what God said. Also, it makes obedience to His instructions easier to carry out. In carrying out God's instructions, you cannot allow yourself to become comfortable with boundaries, or limitations from you or anyone else. At this time the Word that comes is *rhema*, meaning a specific word for a specific time that prompts a God opportunity.

These God opportunities are called *kairos* moments. *Kairos* in the Greek translation means "right or opportune moment." It is used to define a specific time that, actually, exists in-between time as we know it. It is, also, a moment of an undetermined period of time in which something unique and special happens, sometimes referring to time standing still. God does not operate in our time, which in the Greek translation is *chronos*. Time is just an earthly tool or measurement that we use for reference or to track our testimonies. Therefore, God's blessings operate outside of time and can accelerate time as we know it.

Often times, when a prophetic word is released, it must be followed by a prophetic gesture, which is a corresponding action prompted by faith.

Mark 9:1-8

King James Version (KJV)

9 And he said unto them, Verily I say unto you, That there be some of them that stand here, which shall not taste of death, till they have seen the kingdom of God come with power.

2 And after six days Jesus taketh with him Peter, and James, and John, and leadeth them up into an high mountain apart by themselves: and he was transfigured before them.

3 And his raiment became shining, exceeding white as snow; so as no fuller on earth can white them.

4 And there appeared unto them Elias with Moses: and they were talking with Jesus.

5 And Peter answered and said to Jesus, Master, it is good for us to be here: and let us make three tabernacles; one for thee, and one for Moses, and one for Elias.

6 For he wist not what to say; for they were sore afraid.

7 And there was a cloud that overshadowed them: and a voice came out of the cloud, saying, This is my beloved Son: hear him.

⁸ And suddenly, when they had looked round about, they saw no man any more, save Jesus only with themselves.

The prophetic word was, "Arise, take up thy bed, and go unto thine house." The prophetic gesture was, "and he arose, and departed to his house." The *kairos* moment was there, but without the prophetic gesture, destiny could have been delayed, or forfeited. Validating that destiny is a decision.

Kairos moments usually come wrapped up in crisis. Your worst time naturally could be the finest hour for God to activate a portion of your destiny. It is really based on perception. There has to be an internal transformation that establishes a new mind set. Activation always takes place internally before it manifest externally.

Trust God in every stage of the process towards your destiny, and be confident in knowing that He that started a good work in you is faithful to perform it until the day of Jesus Christ. Embrace the journey!

Activation Stage Quote:

> *In order to manifest the destiny that lies inside of you, you cannot be afraid of what lies ahead.*

Notes:

About Rhonda Pettigrew

Author and high impact preacher and teacher, Pastor Rhonda Pettigrew is becoming one of the most sought after voices, not only to churches, but, also in the business, leadership, and mentorship platforms. She is a revolutionary thinker, a difference maker, and a culture shaper.

Pastor Rhonda has traveled throughout the country preaching and leading worship. She served as an International Worship Leader for the Full Gospel Baptist Church Fellowship for seven years, with four years of leading the Central Region as Director of Worship, under the direction of Bishop William Murphy, III and the covering of Bishop Paul S. Morton, Sr.

Pastor Rhonda has been a featured guest on, Trinity Broadcasting Network (TBN) and appeared on The Word Network, The Christian

Broadcasting Network (CBN), as well as many other Christian Television Productions.

Pastor Rhonda's first book, "Manifesting Your Destiny," was released in 2013 with an expanded version released in 2016. Pastor Rhonda has also penned, "The Emerging Leader", a guide for leaders to evolve into their maximum potential.

Pastor Rhonda is married to Pastor Danny Pettigrew. God is using them to be a model for effective team ministry. Together, they founded Destiny Church in Jackson, Tennessee in January 2011. Destiny Church's vision is to impact the lives of people with relevant teaching and personal development in every city, every nation, everyday.

Log on to www.rhondapettigrew.com for booking and more information.